THE SEVEN SAGES OF ANCIENT GREECE

Other philosophical books by Constantine Cavarnos

A DIALOGUE BETWEEN BERGSON, ARISTOTLE, AND PHILOLOGOS

MAN AND THE UNIVERSE IN AMERICAN PHILOSOPHY

MODERN GREEK PHILOSOPHERS ON THE HUMAN SOUL

BYZANTINE THOUGHT AND ART

MODERN GREEK THOUGHT

PLATO'S THEORY OF FINE ART

PLATO'S VIEW OF MAN

THE CLASSICAL THEORY OF RELATIONS

A DIALOGUE ON G.E. MOORE'S ETHICAL PHILOSOPHY

PHILOSOPHICAL STUDIES

THE EDUCATIONAL THEORY OF BENJAMIN OF LESVOS

THE HELLENIC-CHRISTIAN PHILOSOPHICAL TRADITION

PYTHAGORAS ON THE FINE ARTS AS THERAPY

THALES

Wall painting by Photios Kontoglou in the City Hall (*Demarcheion*) of Athens. 1937.

THE SEVEN SAGES OF ANCIENT GREECE

The lives and teachings of the earliest Greek philosophers

Thales • Pittacos • Bias • Solon • Cleobulos • Myson • Chilon

By

CONSTANTINE CAVARNOS

INSTITUTE FOR BYZANTINE
AND MODERN GREEK STUDIES
115 Gilbert Road
Belmont, Massachusetts 02178–2200
U.S.A.

Design & Typesetting by:
E. Marshall Publishing & Translation Services
Brookline, Massachusetts

Second printing, 2017
First edition, 1996

Published by THE INSTITUTE FOR BYZANTINE
AND MODERN GREEK STUDIES, INC.
115 Gilbert Road, Belmont, Massachusetts 02178-220, U.S.A.

Printed in the United States of America

Library of Congress Catalog Number: 96-77300

Clothbound ISBN 1-884729-16-9
Paperbound ISBN 1-884729-17-7

PREFACE

This book had its beginning in a course on the Pre-Socratic Philosophers which I taught many years ago at the University of North Carolina in Chapel Hill, N.C. I discussed then the Seven Sages of Ancient Greece in the early part of the course. In teaching recently the Pre-Socratic Philosophers at the Institute for Byzantine and Modern Greek Studies, I augmented considerably what I had said in that part of the course. The result is the text of the present book.

In preparing it for publication, I thought it useful to add illustrations showing the Wise Men, wherever such illustrations are available, to include a Bibliography and Indexes, and also an Appendix presenting Selected Sayings of the Seven Sages, both in the Greek language in which they have come down to us from early times, and in the English translation which I freshly made of them.

The Selected Sayings have been taken from the two-volume *Treasury of Sacred and Philosophical Sayings* (*Hierón kai Philosophikón Logíon Thesaúrisma*) by St. Nectarios Kephalas, Metropolitan of Pentapolis (1846-1920) that was published in Athens during the years 1894-1895. Nectarios was a distinguished churchman and scholar. He was acquainted with the whole Greek heritage in its uninterrupted continuity from Antiquity to the present. The fact that he included these Sayings in that monumental work, scattered amongst a vast number of statements taken from the Holy Scriptures and the writings of the Eastern Orthodox Church Fathers, shows that he saw an essential harmony between the teachings of these Sages and those of authentic Christianity. And the fact that among his sources of the Sayings, besides the 3rd century A.D. writer Diogenes Laertios, are several nineteenth century Greek writers, shows that the Sayings of the Seven Sages have also been duly appreciated by other notable modern Greek scholars. In his Epilogue, St. Nectarios cites the following modern Greek sources he used in preparing his two-volume work: Neophytos Metaxas' *Hierographikón Apánthisma* ("Anthology of Sacred Writings"), Anastasios Kephalas' *Opsimathés* ("Late in Learning"), Penelope Giallouri's *Kypséle* ("Beehive"), and *Mélissa* ("Bee").

The present book is addressed to all persons who are lovers of perennial wisdom — of wisdom that can serve in every age and every country as a safe guide in one's individual and public life.

CONSTANTINE CAVARNOS

Belmont, Massachusetts
May 1996

CONTENTS

THALES

Ancient bust.

INTRODUCTION

Modern books presenting the history of ancient Greek philosophy begin with the "Milesians,[1] namely, Thales, Anaximander, and Anaximenes. They bypass the Seven Wise Men of Greece completely, or speak of them in a few lines, except for Thales, who is regarded in such histories as the only one of the Seven who was a philosopher. This is true even of recent Greek historians of Greek philosophy, such as Nicholaos Louvaris and K.D. Georgoulis. Louvaris wrote a two-volume *History of Philosophy* (*Historía tes Philosophías*) that was published in Athens in 1933, while Georgoulis wrote a two-volume *History of Greek Philosophy* (*Historía tes Hellenikés Philosophías*), which appeared in print in the same city in 1975.

By contrast, the early Greek historian of Greek philosophy Diogenes Laertios (3rd century A.D.), in

[1] They are so called because they were natives of the Greek city of Miletos, on the west coast of Asia Minor.

presenting a history of Greek philosophy in his book *Lives and Opinions of Eminent Philosophers in Ten Books*, begins his history of Greek philosophy with the Seven Sages and devotes many pages to them. Plato (427-347 B.C.), who was much closer to the Seven Greek Sages in time than was Laertios, speaks of them as *exemplary philosophers.* His account of them is the earliest, most remarkable, and most authoritative one that we have. It appears in his dialogue *Protagoras.* There Plato says:

"Thales of Miletos, Pittacos of Mytilene, Bias of Priene, Solon of Athens, Cleobulos of Lindos, Myson of Chen, and the last of the traditional seven, Chilon the Lacedaemonian [Spartan], all were zealots, lovers and disciples of the *Spartan* culture (*paideía*). And you can perceive clearly that their culture was of such a nature by the short (*brachéa*), noteworthy sayings that were uttered by each of them. These sayings, when they assembled together, they dedicated as the firstfruits of their wisdom (*sophía*) to Apollo in his temple at Delphi, inscribing there those sayings which everyone repeats: *'Know thyself'* (*Gnóthi Sautón*) and *'Nothing to excess'* (*Medén*

Agan)."[2]

This passage is ascribed by Plato to his great teacher Socrates, the leading character in the *Protagoras* and Plato's mouthpiece. Then Plato has Socrates add this:

"Why do I say these things? In order to show that this was the style of the *ancient philosophers*: a

---

[2] 343A-B. The wisdom and importance of the maxim "Know thyself" has been duly appreciated in the Hellenic Christian East from the early centuries of the Christian era down to our time. Thus, Clement of Alexandria (*ca.* 150-211/215) says in his *Paidagogós* (Instructor): "It is then, as appears, the greatest of all lessons to know one's self. For if one knows himself, he will know God; and knowing God, he will be made like God by well-doing, and by requiring as few things as possible" (*The Ante-Nicene Fathers*, Vol. II, p. 271). And St. Nectarios, Metropolitan of Pentapolis (1846-1920), remarks: "Thales the Milesian held that self-knowledge is the beginning of every virtue. Therefore, it is necessary that we know ourselves, in order that we might become virtuous. For knowledge of ourselves will be our guide leading us to virtue. The man who knows himself knows that he is a rational, spiritual being, possessing the power of free choice and self-control, and hence religious, social, ethical, and in his spiritual nature immortal" (*Perí tes Alethoús kai Pseudoús Morphóseos* ["Concerning True and Pseudo Education"]. Athens, 1894, p. 8).

certain Laconic *brevity in speech* (*brachylogía*)."[3]

Significant is the fact that the Platonic Socrates calls all the above-mentioned Seven Wise men *philosophers*, and praises them for their *brachylogía*, their style of making notable remarks short and compressed.

After mentioning the two sayings which all Seven Sages agreed to have inscribed at the temple of Apollo at Delphi, Plato adds a third important one, which he ascribes to Pittacos of Mytilene. The saying is this: "It is hard to be good (*Chalepón esthlón émmenai*)."[4] What Pittacos meant was that in order to become good, struggle is needed, persistent efforts, an upward path of moral endeavor.

Regarding the first two sayings, the noted Hellenist Kathleen Freeman has aptly remarked that they acquired importance in later *philosophy* thanks to the work of Socrates, Plato, and Aristotle. "Socrates developed '*Know thyself*' into 'Virtue is knowledge,' and Plato and Aristotle developed '*Nothing*

---

[3] *Protagoras*, 343B.

[4] 343 B.C.

too much' into the doctrine of the [Golden] Mean."[5]

Demetrios of Phaleron — a fourth century B.C. statesman, orator, philosopher, and poet — made a collection of sayings of the Seven Sages. These "lay stress on the moral virtues of *self-control, honesty, industry, truthfulness, obedience to the laws, respect towards parents, and common sense in general* . . . They were intended as a practical guide to life."[6]

Diogenes Laertios presents such sayings in his accounts of the Seven Wise Men, taking them from Demetrios and other early Greek writers. From these sayings and what Plato says in the *Protagoras* about the Seven Wise Men, it is evident that their contribution to philosophy was chiefly in the fields of *ethics* and *legislation,* and in the *laconic style* which they cultivated and through their wise sayings bequeathed to later philosophers. Plato and Socrates, as we saw, were great admirers of that style, which they termed *brachylogía.* It served as a precious lesson to them. They opposed it to the prolix style of the Sophists, who were contemporaries of theirs.

---

[5] *The Pre-Socratic Philosophers,* 1946, p. 45.

[6] *Ibid.* The italics are mine.

Plato calls that style *makrología,* "long speech."[7] In the *Protagoras,* at one point in the discussion about virtue, after the Sophist Protagoras delivered a long speech in answer to a question by Socrates, the latter tells Protagoras: "Protagoras, if you are going to continue the discussion with me, you will have to follow the style of *brevity* (*brachylogía*)."[8]

Hippias, one of the other Sophists present, describes Socrates' style as one characterized by *precision* (*to akribés*) and extreme brevity (*to katá brachý lían*).[9] It is evident from what is said in Plato's dialogue that Socrates adhered to the style of brief questions and answers in his philosophical discussions. That Plato used this style is evident in all his dialogues. Thus, both these great philosophers not only *admired the brachylogía* taught by the Seven Wise Men, but also faithfully *practiced* it. Plato's greatest disciple — Aristotle — also employed *brachylogía.* His style has been characterized by moderns as "elliptical." A recent writer observes

---

[7] *Protagoras,* 335B, 336B.

[8] *Ibid.,* 335A.

[9] *Ibid.,* 337E-348A.

that Aristotle's writings are characterized by "terse enunciations, beautiful indeed in their precision, but strangely cramped in their linguistic form."[10]

---

[10] Margorie Grene, *A Portrait of Aristotle,* Chicago, 1963, p. 49. Photios Kontoglou has noted *brachylogía* in a number of nineteenth century Greek writers: General Makrygiannis, Kasomoulis, Kolokotronis, Photakos, Palaion Patron Germanos, and certain others. Their historical narratives, he remarks, are written "with economy of time, of paper, of ink, and of imagination" (C. Cavarnos, *Meetings with Kontoglou,* Belmont, MA, 1992, pp. 71-72). *Brachylogía* is also characteristic of the nineteenth century Greek poet Andreas Kalvos and the narrative writer Alexandros Papadiamantis, of the twentieth century Greek poets Constantine Cavafy and George Seferis, of Photios Kontoglou himself, and of other Greek writers of the recent past.

1

THALES

The first known Greek Philosopher and Scientist

Thales (624-545 B.C.) was the first to receive the name of "sage" or "wise man" (*sophós*). He was a native of Miletos, a city on the western coast of Asia Minor, in the region known as Ionia. At that time Ionia was part of Greece.

It is not known whether he put down his views in writing. If he did, his writings did not long survive. What we know about him and his teaching is based on what other ancient Greek authors have written about him and his views. They say that he was the first among the Greeks *to study astronomy,* the first *to predict eclipses* of the sun, the first *to discuss physical problems* — that is, problems about the nature of the physical world — and the first to say that *the soul is immortal.*[1]

Although Thales is said to have lived in solitude (*monéres*), he is also said to have taken interest in political matters and to have given excellent advice regarding them.

Some ancient writers say that he was married and had a son, while others say that he never married. There is a story that when his mother tried to force him to marry, Thales replied that it was too early, and when later she pressed him again, he replied that it was too late.

Nothing is known about his Greek teachers. He is said to have gone to Egypt and spent some time with the priests, who were the most learned class in Egypt. From this association, it is said, he learned geometry.

Two remarkable anecdotes regarding Thales have come down to us, one revealing his ability to grow rich if he wanted to, and the other showing his philosophical nature. The first anecdote, as

---

[1] Diogenes Laertios, *Lives and Opinions of Eminent Philosophers*, Loeb Classical Library, Vol. I. 24. For brevity, I shall often refer to this writer as simply "Diogenes."

related by the philosopher Hieronymos of Rhodes (4th-3rd centuries B.C.), a disciple of Aristotle, is as follows: "Once, foreseeing that it would be a good season for olives, Thales rented all the oil-mills and thus (having created a monopoly, and therefore being able to charge what he pleased) amassed a fortune."[2] Aristotle remarks that Thales thus "proved that it is easy for philosophers to be rich if they choose, but this is not what they care about."[3] Diogenes says that Thales did this simply to show that it is possible to become rich easily.

The second anecdote, as described by Plato in his dialogue *Theaetetus*, is as follows: "While Thales was studying the stars and looking upward, he fell into a well, and a graceful, witty Thracian servant girl jeered at him, it is said, because he was so eager to know the things in heaven that he could not see what was before his feet." Plato remarks that "the same jest applies to all who pass their lives in philosophy."[4]

---

[2] Diogenes, *op. cit.*, I. 26-27.

[3] Aristotle, *Politics*, I. 1259a.

[4] *Theatetus*, 174A-B.

The true philosopher — and Thales is cited as an example of such a philosopher — explains Plato, "disdains the things that engross the attention of the many, considering them as things petty and of no account. Instead, he turns his mind to the investigation of the universal nature of everything that is. Thus, he inquires and exerts himself to find out what a human being is and what is proper for such a nature to do or bear different from any other."[5]

There is an allusion in the last statement to the proverb "Know thyself," which is attributed to Thales, and which Plato says was inscribed by the Seven Wise Men on the temple at Delphi. Plato explains here how this famous saying is to be understood.

One may ask, if a human being's most important quest should be to know himself, why did Thales himself spend time looking up to the firmament of heaven and studying the stars? And if Plato himself agreed with Thales on the importance of the quest for self-knowledge, why did he say that true philosopher turns his mind to the investigation of

---

[5] *Ibid.*, 174B.

the universal nature *of everything that is*? The answer is as follows:

To attain genuine knowledge about the nature and destiny of man is a most difficult task. For it is impossible to discern the nature of the soul (which chiefly constitutes man) unless one has studied and learned what is true and what is false of the whole of existence. The knowledge that is needed of man is not of man as an isolated being, as an abstraction, but as an integral being, in all his significant relations to reality as a whole. Thus, to treat of man the philosopher must treat of the whole of reality. He must acquire a knowledge and understanding of *the whole universe.*[6]

Another very interesting and didactic anecdote, one pertains to Thales as well as to the other six Wise Men of Greece, is about a tripod. Diogenes Laertios has a great deal to say about this in speaking of these men. Kathleen Freeman sums up the stories about the tripod as follows:

---

[6] See my book *Plato's View of Man*, Belmont, MA, 1975, 1982, p. 16.

"A golden tripod was drawn out of the sea by some fishermen of Kos or Miletos. When a dispute arose over its ownership, the Pythia [of Delphi] was appealed to, and the reply was: 'Give it to the wisest of all.' First it was sent to Thales, according to Plutarch, and Thales sent it to Bias. It passed to each of the Wise Men in turn until it came back to Thales, who sent it to Thebes, as a gift to the Ismenian Apollo. There are many variations of the story. Theophrastos[7] [of Lesvos] said that Bias [of Priene, Asia Minor] was the first and last to receive it, and that he sent it to Delphi . . . Another version of the story is that the golden tripod was sent to Thales first, and Solon last; and that it was Solon who realized the meaning of the Oracle, and sent it to Delphi."[8]

Freeman remarks that the theme of the story is the modesty of the Seven Wise Men and their admiration for one another. It seems to me that the anecdote is intended to show (a) the *intellectual humility* of Thales and the other Wise Men, each one

---

[7] 371-288 B.C.

[8] *The Work and Life of Solon,* Cardiff, 1926, p. 196.

considering himself less wise than the other, and (b) that they believed that God far surpasses all humans in wisdom.

Many apophthegms have been ascribed to Thales. Among them are the following:

"Of all things that are, the most ancient is God, for he is a being uncreated (*agénetos*)."

"The most beautiful is the universe, for it is God's workmanship."

"The greatest is space, for it contains all things."

"The swiftest is mind (*nous*), for it speeds everywhere."

"Be beautiful in your conduct."

These sayings are quoted by Diogenes in his account of Thales.[9] He found them assigned to Thales by some other authors, whom he does not name.

That Thales believed in a supreme God has been viewed as attested to by the statement ascribed to him, and often mentioned in histories of philosophy, that "All things are full of gods." Regarding this, the

---

[9] *Op. cit.*, I. 35-36.

eminent English historian of Greek philosophy John Burnet says:

"This statement is supposed by Aristotle to imply that Thales believed in a 'soul of the world' . . . The doctrine of the world-soul is then attributed quite positively to Thales by Aetios [later than 4th century B.C.] . . . who identifies the world-intellect with God. Cicero [106-43 B.C.] goes a step further. Eliminating the Stoic pantheism, he turns the world-intellect into the Platonic *Demiourgós,* and says that Thales held there was a divine mind which formed all things."[10]

The Athenian philosopher and Christian Apologist Athenagoras (2nd century) similarly attributes to Thales the belief in the existence of a Supreme God, a World-Intelligence. Thus, in his work *Plea for the Christians,* Athenagoras says: "Thales, as those who have accurately examined his opinions report, divides superior beings into God, demons, and heroes. God he recognizes as the Intelligence (*Nous*) of the world; by demons he understands beings possessed of soul (*psychikaí*); and by heroes the

---

[10] Burnet, *Early Greek Philosophy,* London, 1920, pp. 49-50.

separated souls of men, the good being the good souls, and the bad being the worthless [ones]."[11]

Diogenes lists various questions that were put to Thales and the answers he gave to them. Among these are the following:

"How shall I lead the best life." His answer: "By refraining from doing what we blame in others." To the question "What man is happy (*eudaímon*)?" he replied: "That individual who has a healthy body, a resourceful mind, and a nature that is well-educated."[12]

The most famous saying ascribed to Thales, as well as to the other Greek Wise Men, is: "Know thyself." He is said to have regarded self-knowledge as difficult to achieve (*Dyskolon to heautón gnónai*)."

Thales was a man of practical wisdom not only in the sphere of *ethics*, but also in that of *politics*.

---

[11] *The Ante-Nicene Fathers*, Vol. II, p. 141. The word "demon" did not have in ancient Greek writings the meaning it has in Holy Scripture, namely, of an evil spiritual being. It meant a "god." Thus, when Thales said that "the world is full of *daímones*" (Diogenes, *op. cit.*, I. 27), he did not mean that it was full of evil spiritual beings, but of divine ones.

[12] Diogenes, *op. cit.*, I. 36-37.

Plato praises him for his political sagacity, through which he contributed in very concrete ways to the well-being of his fellow-citizens.[13] He was a wise lawgiver (*nomothétes*), and offered excellent advice on political matters. For instance, "when Croesus sent persons to Miletos offering terms of alliance, he (Thales) frustrated the plan; and this proved the salvation of the city when Cyrus obtained victory."[14] Also, he is said to have offered a plan for the union of the twelve Ionian city-states to form a federation, but his advice was not heeded.

The Milesian philosopher was a man also well-versed in science. He is reputed to have introduced geometry into Greece;[15] and of his knowledge of astronomy there is no doubt. He is credited with having predicted the eclipse of the sun which took place on May 28, 585 B.C.[16] This prediction contrib-

---

[13] *Republic*, X. 600A.

[14] Diogenes, *op. cit.*, I. 25.

[15] Herodotos, II. 20. Cf. Ivor Thomas, *Greek Mathematics from Thales to Euclid*, Loeb Classical Library, Vol. I, pp. 164-169.

[16] E. Zeller, *Outlines of the History of Greek Philosophy*, London and New York, 1895, p. 38.

uted greatly to his becoming famous. Some have held that he wrote a work *On Nautical Astronomy* — that is, astronomy for sailors — one *On the Solstice,* and one *On the Equinox.*[17]

He is unique among the Seven Wise of Greece in that his philosophic interest extended not only to science, but also to the field of metaphysics.[18] He is reputed to have asked for the first time in Greece the question: "What is the basic stuff out of which all things are made and into which they resolve?" His answer to this question was that the basic stuff or substance is water (*hydor*).

Why did Thales choose water as his fundamental explanatory principle? Aristotle saw the influence of Greek mythology in Thales' choice. "There are some," says Aristotle, "who think that the men of very ancient times, long before the present era, who first speculated about the gods, also held

---

[17] *Op. cit.,* I. 23.

[18] Cf. Plutarch: "It would seem that Thales was the only Wise Man of the time who carried his speculations beyond the realm of the practical. The rest got the name of wisdom from their excellence as statesmen" (*Parallel Lives,* Loeb Classical Library, Vol. I, pp. 411-413).

this same opinion about the primary entity. For they represented Oceanus and Tethys to be the parents of creation, and the oath of the gods to be water."[19] Aristotle has an additional suggestion. Thales, he remarks, might have arrived at his view by the twofold observation that the germ cells or seeds of all living things are of a moist nature, and also that the nourishment of all things is moist.[20]

It seems likely that Thales was also led to adopt water as the basic substance by the following observation: We note that water can pass through all the states which physical objects can assume: water can exist as a *liquid,* as a *gas,* and as a *solid* (ice, snow). This means that one and the same substance, water, passes through various states and yet remains essentially the same. Hence, water seems to be the *one* in the *many* changing things.

Thales' question, "What is the basic stuff out of which all things are made?" served as the starting point of subsequent philosophical speculations to answer this question. Later Greek philosophers

---

[19] *Metaphysics,* I. 983b30-34.

[20] *Ibid.,* I. 983b18-27.

implicitly agreed that Thales had asked a very important question. However, they thought that he had not given the right answer. Thus, we see one of them asserting that the basic stuff is not water but *air* (Anaximenes); another holding that it is *fire* (Heracleitos); another maintaining that it is none of these but the *infinite* (Anaximander); and still another stating that there is *not one* basic substance: there are four: *earth, water, air,* and *fire* (Empedocles). A recent philosopher, Bertrand Russell, has made the following interesting and noteworthy remark on Thales' view: "The statement that everything is made of water is to be regarded as a scientific hypothesis, and by no means a foolish one. Twenty years ago, the received view was that everything is made of hydrogen, which is two-thirds water."[21]

---

[21] *A History of Western Philosophy*. New York, 1945, p. 26.

2

PITTACOS

Statesman and Ruler of Mytilene

Pittacos (*ca.* 650–*ca.* 570 B.C.) is mentioned by Plato immediately after Thales in his list of the Seven Wise Men of Greece. He was a native of Mytilene, the capital of Lesvos. This island is in the northeastern part of the Aegean Sea, near the coast of Asia Minor. The people of Mytilene greatly honored Pittacos and entrusted him with the office of governing the city. "He ruled Mytilene for ten years, and brought the constitution (*políteuma*) to order."[1] J. Irving Manatt, who was professor of Greek at Brown University, has this to say about Pittacos' rule:

---

[1] Diogenes, *op. cit.*, I. 75.

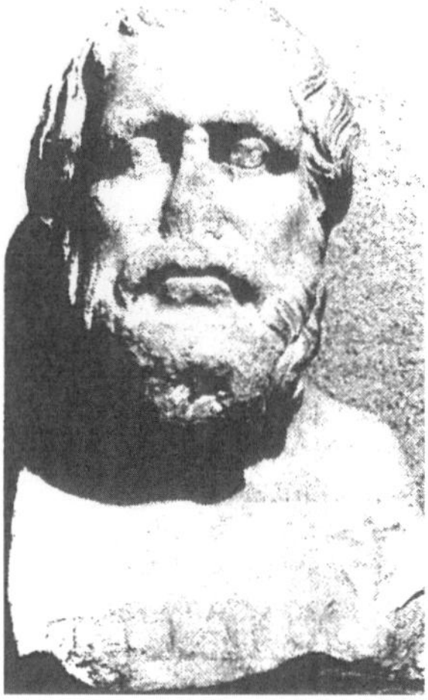

PITTACOS
Bust, Louvre Museum, Paris.

PITTACOS
Relief on a copper coin
of Lesvos.

"In Sappho's day the struggle of the classes — to which she and Alkaios belonged — and the masses was in full swing; the rigorous rule of an old nobility bred the demagogue and the demagogue evolved the tyrant until at last the people found in sage Pittakos a man to heal the discord and restore the state."[2]

Pamphile, a woman historian of the first century A.D., relates in her *Memorabilia* that Pittacos forgave the murderer of his son Tyrraios and set him free, saying: "Forgiveness (*sygnóme*) is better than regret."[3] The philosopher Heracleitos (535-475 B.C.) gave a different version of the event that showed Pittacos' exemplary forgiveness. He said that it was the poet Alkaios (Alcaeus) whom Pittacos set free, at the time when he got Alkaios in his power; and that what Pittacos said was: "Forgiveness is better

---

[2] J. Irving Manatt, *Aegean Days*, Boston, 1914, p. 298. Cf. Aristotle: "There is concord in a state when the citizens unanimously decree that the office of state shall be elective, or that an alliance shall be made with Sparta, or that Pittacos shall be ruler — when Pittacos was himself willing to be ruler" (*Nichomachean Ethics*, IX, 1167A).

[3] Diogenes, *op. cit.*, I. 76.

than vengeance."[4] Both versions of the incident of forgiveness show that Pittacos was noble-minded, a man who had the virtue of forgiveness to an eminent degree.

Diogenes ascribes to Pittacos *poems* in elegiac metre, some 600 lines, and a prose work *On Laws* for the use of the citizens.[5]

One of the remarkable laws which he is said to have made provided that for any offense committed in a state of intoxication the penalty should be doubled. There should be one penalty for the offense and one in order to prevent excessive drinking. "His object was to discourage drunkenness."[6] Aristotle approved of this law in his *Nicomachean Ethics*.[7] The well-governed State seeks to *teach* its citizens that certain acts are evil, and to *dissuade* people from performing such acts. Aristotle emphasized the value of *state laws as educators* of the people, teaching them what is right and what is

---

[4] *Ibid.*

[5] *Ibid.*, I. 78.

[6] *Ibid.*, I. 76.

[7] III. 1113b 30-35.

wrong, inducing them to do what is good and dissuading them from doing what is evil.[8]

Among the sagacious sayings attributed to Pittacos[9] are the following:

"It is hard to be good (*Chalepón esthlón émmenai*)." Plato discusses this saying at some length in his dialogue *Protagoras*.[10] He remarks that Pittacos meant that it is hard to *become* good, requiring struggle.

"Office (*arché*) shows the man." The meaning of this saying seems to be that the possession of office or authority makes manifest whether a person is just or unjust, wise or unwise, gentle or ruthless.

"It is the part of prudent men, before difficulties arise, to provide against their arising; and of courageous men to deal with them when they have arisen.

"Speak no ill of friend, nor yet of an enemy." This saying is somewhat like Christ's commandment to love one's neighbor, including one's enemies:

---

[8] *Nichomachean Ethics*, X. 1179B 30ff.

[9] Diogenes, *op. cit.*, I. 77-78.

[10] 345E ff.

"Love your enemies and bless them that hate you."[11]

"Practice piety" (*eusébeia*).

"Love temperance (*sophrosyne*), truth, fidelity, experience, skill, sociability, diligence." In this passage the virtues of *temperance* and *love of truth* are emphasized by being mentioned first. "Temperance" for the ancient Greeks meant self-mastery, manifested in the avoidance of the evils of excess on the one hand and of deficiency (lack) on the other hand. When the Seven Wise Men said "*Medén ágan*" ("Nothing to excess"), with these two words they were exhorting people to cultivate this very important and beautiful quality.

The love of truth (*philalétheia*), which the same passage exhorts people to cultivate, was one of the distinctive characteristics of the classical Greek philosophers. Seraphim of Sarov, the great Russian saint of the last century, took notice of this. Thus he said: "The pagan philosophers, although they wandered in the darkness of ignorance of the Deity, yet sought the *truth* which is beloved of God. By this very God-pleasing search they were enabled to

[11] *Matthew*, 5:44.

partake of the Spirit of God."[12]

The best known apophthegm of Pittacos is the laconic, two-word counsel: *Kairón gnóthi,* "Know thine opportune time."[13] The point of this saying is that opportunities of various kinds appear at certain points in one's lifetime, and that individual succeeds who, being watchful and discerning, sees these opportunities at the time when they arise and promptly seizes them.

Some ancient writers say that Pittacos was a teacher of the philosopher Pherekydes of Syros, who in turn was a teacher of the philosopher Pythagoras.[14]

In the light of the account concerning Pittacos that I have given in this chapter, we may safely conclude that Plato spoke rightly when he characterized Pittacos as "wise and blessed."[15]

---

[12] Constantine Cavarnos and Mary-Barbara Zeldin, *St. Seraphim of Sarov,* Vol. 5 of the series *Modern Orthodox Saints,* Belmont, MA, 1980, p. 105.

[13] Diogenes, *op. cit.,* I. 79.

[14] Kathleen Freeman, *The Pre-Socratic Philosophers,* 1946, p. 36.

[15] *Republic,* I. 335E.

BIAS

Bust in the Museum
of the Vatican.

3

BIAS

Orator and Judge

Bias, pronounced in Greek *Vias* (*ca.* 625–*ca.* 540 B.C.), the third in Plato's list of the Seven Wise Men, was born in Priene, a city in Ionia north of Miletos.

According to Diogenes Laertios, "Bias wrote a poem of 2,000 lines on Ionia and the manner of rendering it prosperous."[1] The most popular lines of those that were sung are the following:

"Be agreeable to all the citizens,
  in whatever city you dwell.
For this earns the most favor,
  whereas the uncourteous manner
  often flashes forth harmful defeat.

---

[1] *Op. cit.*, I. 85.

Diogenes ascribes to Bias many other sayings, such as these:[2]

"To set forth in speech the interests of one's country is a gift of the soul and of wisdom."

"Hope (*elpís*) is sweet to men."

"It is a disease of the soul (*nósos psychés*) to be enamored of things impossible of attainment."

"Be slow to set about an enterprise, but persevere in it strongly when once it is undertaken."

"Do not be hasty in speech (*me tachý lálei*), for that manifests madness."

"Gain your point by persuasion, not by force."

"If a man is unworthy, do not praise him because of his wealth."

"Attribute to the gods whatever good acts you perform." This precept tends to inculcate the virtues of humility and piety. It has a Christian parallel in the Epistle of the Apostle James, when he says: "Every good gift and every perfect gift is from above, and cometh down from the Father of Lights" (1: 17). Although Bias speaks as a polytheist, while

---

[2] *Ibid.*, 86-88.

James speaks as a Christian monotheist, both are in accord in recognizing the existence of a divine personal reality that cares for men and helps them in their efforts to do good.

"Love Wisdom."

"Make wisdom your provision for the journey from youth to old age; for it is a more certain support than all your possessions." This counsel and the immediately preceding one show clearly that Bias was truly a philosopher, an individual enamored of wisdom.

St. Basil the Great cites an anecdote about Bias which contains a counsel akin to the preceding. He says: "Bias when asked by his son who was about to depart for Egypt, what he could do that would gratify him most, replied, 'By acquiring travel-supplies for your old age,' meaning by 'travel supplies,' no doubt, virtue."[3]

Aristotle ascribes to Bias a saying which, as we saw, Diogenes attributes to Pittacos: "Office will show a man." He remarks: "We approve this saying

---

[3] *To Young Men on How They Might Derive Profit from Greek Literature*, X.

of Bias, for in office one is brought into relation with others and becomes a member of a community."[4] What "office" will show, according to Aristotle, is whether one can practice the virtue of justice in *public affairs*. For he notes that "there are many who can practice virtue in their own private affairs but cannot do so in their relations with others."[5] Aristotle obviously esteemed Bias' wisdom. So did Plato, Aristotle's great teacher. In the first book of the *Republic* he praises Bias, along with Pittacos, as a "wise and blessed man." An earlier philosopher, Heracleitos (535-475 B.C.), also had very high regard for Bias. He wrote: "In Priene lived Bias, a man of more consideration than any others."[6]

[4] *Nichomachean Ethics*, V. 1130al-3.

[5] *Ibid.*, 1129b30-35.

[6] Diogenes, *op. cit.*, I. 88.

4

SOLON

Lawgiver, Founder of Athenian Democracy, and Poet

Solon, whose name has become synonymous with "lawgiver," was born around 630 B.C. at Salamis, an island near Piraeus, the port of Athens. He died in Cyprus at the age of about seventy.

Diogenes Laertios begins his account of Solon by noting his first achievement as a lawgiver. This was "the Law of Release," which he introduced at Athens. "Its effect was to ransom persons and property. For men used to borrow money on personal security, and many were forced from poverty to become serfs or day laborers. He then first renounced his claim to a debt of seven talents due to his father, and encouraged others to follow his example."[1]

---

[1] Diogenes, *op. cit.*, I. 45.

SOLON
Ancient bust.

Another admirable law which he enacted was that "if any man neglects to provide for his parents, he shall be disfranchised," that is, deprived of the privileges of a citizen. Still another one was that of "depriving open profligates (*ásotoi*) of the right to speak in the assembly."[2]

Like Pittacos of Mytilene, Solon was strongly against drunkenness, and sought to stop it. Thus, one of his laws was that the magistrate (*archon*) found intoxicated should be punished with death.

Solon enacted these laws in 594 B.C., when he was ruler (*archon*) at Athens. Having enacted them, according to Herodotos, "he left his home for ten years and set out on a voyage to see the world, as he said. This he did, lest he should be compelled to repeal any of the laws he had made, since the Athenians themselves could not repeal them, for they were bound by solemn oaths to abide for ten years by such laws as Solon should make."[3]

When he was asked how crime could most effectively be diminished, he replied: "If it caused as

---

[2] *Ibid.*, 55.

[3] Herodotos, Book I. 29.

much resentment in those who are not its victims as in those who are."

Solon regarded tragic dramas as pernicious, as did Plato who flourished at a later time. Thus, when Pesistratos appeared with self-inflicted wounds, Solon ascribed this to the influence of such dramas.

Like the other Wise Men I have discussed — Thales, Pittacos, and Bias — Solon is credited with counsels to men in general. Diogenes cites the following, which he found in Apollodoros' work on the *Philosophic Sects*:

"Put more trust in goodness of character (*kalokagathía*) than on oath."

"Do not tell lies (*Me pseudou*)."

"Direct your attention to good ends."

"Learn to obey before you rule."

"In giving advice seek to help, not to please, your friend."

"Make reason (*nous*) your ruler."

"Avoid bad company."

"Honor the gods and reverence your parents."[4]

---

[4] Diogenes, *op. cit.*, 1-60.

The last counsel gives evidence that Solon was a pious man.

Clement of Alexandria (ca. 150-215), the first known Christian scholar, has expressed high esteem for some verses written by Solon. In his *Stromateis,* Clement says: "The Athenian Solon most excellently writes:

'You look on no good work that has been done;
But each one of you walks in the steps of
  a fox,
And in all of you is an empty mind.'"[5]

Another great early Christian writer of the East, St. Basil, attributes to Solon the following remark about virtue: "We will not exchange with them our virtue for their wealth, since the one abides always, while riches change their owners every day."[6] Commenting on this, St. Basil says: "Other possessions no more belong to their possessors than to any chance comer whatever, quickly shifting now here, now there, as in a game of dice; but virtue alone of

---

[5] Book I, chapter IV.

[6] *Address to Young Men on How They Might Derive Profit from Greek Literature,* V.

possessions cannot be taken away, as it remains with a man whether he be living or dead."

It is said that Solon was the author of the famous apophthegm "Nothing to excess."

In addition to laws and general counsels, Solon is credited with other kinds of writings: speeches, counsels addressed to himself, poems in elegiac and in iambic metre, epodes, on Salamis, and on the Athenian constitution.[7]

The thought and work of Solon have been discussed in many books in various languages — Greek, Latin, English, French, German, Italian, etc. Among the publications in the English language is a book by Kathleen Freeman, entitled *The Work and Life of Solon, With a Translation of his Poems*,[8] and a monograph by John E. Rexine, entitled *Solon and His Political Theory*.[9] This has the subtitle: "The Contemporary Significance of a Basic Contribution to Political Theory by one of the Seven Wise Men."

---

[7] Diogenes, *op. cit.*, I. 61.

[8] Cardiff, 1926.

[9] New York, 1958.

Plato thought very highly of Solon. There are far more references to Solon in his dialogues than to any of the other Sages. He refers to him in the following: *Charmides, Protagoras, Phaedrus, Symposium, Republic, Laches, Timaeus, Critias, Statesman,* and *Laws*. In the *Phaedrus* he characterizes Solon as a philosopher and a good orator, and ascribes to him "political compositions which he called laws."[10] In the *Republic* he remarks: "The Athenians credit Solon with having been a good legislator who benefitted them."[11]

Aristotle, too, shows due appreciation of Solon as a moralist and legislator. In the *Eudemian Ethics* he remarks: "Solon's advice holds good, not to call a man happy while he is alive, but only when he has reached the end, for nothing incomplete is happy, since it is not a whole."[12] And in the *Nichomachean Ethics* he says: "Solon gave a good description of happiness, when he said that in his opinion those men are happy who being moderately

---

[10] 258B.

[11] X. 599E.

[12] II. 1219b.

equipped with external goods, had performed noble exploits and had lived temperately; for it is possible for a man of but moderate possessions to do what is right."[13] The first of these passages is based on a story about Solon's meeting with Croesus, king of Lydia, contained in the first book of Herodotos' *History,* sections 29 to 34. Croesus thought that he himself was the happiest man in the world because he was extremely wealthy and possessed great power. He asked Solon to tell him if he had ever seen a man more blest than he. Solon answered that he had, and cited two examples, men whose lives ended in glorious deaths. And he concluded: Croesus, if I am to speak to you, I say that I see you very rich and the king of many men. But I cannot yet answer your question, before I hear that you have ended your life well."

Aristotle allots considerable space to Solon as a legislator in his book *The Athenian Constitution,* sections v-xiv.[14] His discussion of Solon as a lawgiv-

---

[13] X. 1179a.

[14] Aristotle, *The Athenian Constitution, etc.,* in The Loeb Classical Library.

giver and governor of Athens begins with the following passage: "Such being the system in the Athenian constitution, and the many being enslaved to the few, the people rose against the notables. The party struggle being violent and the parties remaining arrayed in opposition to one another for a long time, they jointly chose Solon as arbitrator and Archon, and entrusted the government to him, after he had composed the political elegy that beings:

> 'I mark, and sorrow fills my breast to see,
> Ionia's oldest land being done to death.'"[15]

Aristotle particularly emphasized that Solon exhorted the wealthy not to be covetous, and he always attached the blame for the civil strife wholly to the rich.[16]

Plutarch, too, was a great admirer of Solon. Thus, he remarks: "Solon was admittedly a lover of wisdom (*sophías erastés*). Even when he was well on in years, he would say that he grew old ever learning many things . . . . In philosophy he cultivated

---

[15] *Ibid.*, V.

[16] *Ibid.*

chiefly the wisdom of political ethics (*tou ethikoú to politikón*), like most of the wise men of the time.... He was not an admirer of wealth, and classed himself among the poor rather than the rich." About Solon's writings, Plutarch says: His early poetry seems to have been composed "as amusement and diversion in his hours of leisure. Later he put philosophic maxims into verse, and interwove many political teachings in his poems."[17]

Solon has always been admired in the Hellenic East for his virtues, especially his wisdom in the sphere of personal and public ethics. In the period of Turkish rule, Greek iconographers sometimes painted Solon, together with other ancient Greeks who had distinguished themselves by their wisdom and other virtues — such as Plato, Aristotle, Plutarch, Sophocles, and Thucydides — in the narthex of churches.[18] In his *Treasury of Sacred and Philosophical Sayings*, St. Nectarios of Pentapolis (1946-1920), the greatest of recent Greek Orthodox saints,

---

[17] Plutarch, *Lives*, Loeb Classical Library, Vol. I, pp. 407, 409, 411.

[18] See Photios Kontoglou, *Ekphrasis of Orthodox Iconography*, Athens, 1960, Vol. 1, pp. 308-309.

has included thirteen sayings of Solon. And the distinguished Abbot of the Monastery of Dionysiou at Mount Athos Father Gabriel (d. 1983) has written this about the Athenian sage: "Solon has been called wiser than the wise for his really wise apophthegm regarding the best State. He said that the best State is that in which the citizens respect the rulers, and the rulers themselves observe the laws."[19]

[19] *The Voice of One Crying from the Wilderness* (*Phoné Boóntos ek tes Erémou*), Volos, 1955, p. 13.

5

CLEOBULOS

Ruler of Lindos and Poet

The four Greek Wise Men whom I have discussed: Thales, Pittacos, Bias, and Solon are included in all enumerations of the Seven Wise Men by ancient Greek writers. The most frequently listed of the rest are Cleobulos, Myson, Chilon, Periander, and Anacharsis. Following Plato's listing,[1] I shall discuss Cleobulos, Myson, and Chilon. The account given of them by Diogenes Laertios, here my chief source, is briefer than those he gives of the already treated four. Hence what I will say about each one of them will be correspondingly shorter.

Cleobulos, a native and ruler of Lindos in Rhodes — one of the Dodecanese Islands in the

---

[1] *Protagoras*, 343A.

Aegean Sea — was in his prime around 600 B.C. Diogenes says that Cleobulos "was the author of songs (*ásmata*) and riddles (*gríphoi*), making some 3,000 lines altogether."[2] In one of his songs, the most popular, he says:

"Want of culture (*amousía*) reigns most widely among mortals, and a multitude of words (*lógon pléthos*), while due measure pleases. Set your mind on something good. Do not be vain and disagreeable."[3]

Implicit in the song is Cleobulos' disapproval of superfluity of words — a commendation of brevity of speech (*brachylogía*), one of the distinguishing characteristics of the Seven Wise Men.

Cleobulos emphasized the need of educating girls as well as boys, saying that parents should give their daughters to their husbands virgins in age but women in wisdom.

Among the other counsels which he offered in his epigrammetic songs were the following:

---

[2] *Op., cit.*, I. 89.

[3] *Ibid.*, 91.

We should do good to a friend to bind him closer to us, and good to an enemy to make a friend of him. (This is similar to Christ's commandment to love not only our friends but also our enemies.)

We should exercise our body (*to sóma askeín*).

We should be fond of listening rather than of talking. (This is in the spirit of Cleobulos' song.)

We should refrain from inauspicious words.

We should be fond of learning.

We should love virtue and hate vice, such as injustice.

We should avoid being overcome by pleasure.

We should do nothing by violence.

We should put an end to enmity.

We should not become proud in prosperity; and when we fall into poverty we should bear it with nobility.

The apophthegm which Diogenes ascribes to Cleobulos is this:

"Moderation is best (*Métron áriston*)."[4]

---

[4] *Ibid.*, I. 93.

That Cleobulos was active in religion is testified to by the tradition that he rebuilt the temple of Athena that was founded by Danaus.

The philosopher Plutarch, who wrote a remarkable *Symposium of the Seven Wise Men,* among whom he includes Cleobulos, attributes to him a strong interest in matters of a political nature and settled views on some of them. Thus, he has Cleobulos say:

"The law, like a weaver, assigns to each one of us so much as is fitting, reasonable, and suitable. It is like the good physician, who in prescribing diet, regimen, and medicines for the sick, does not apportion an equal amount to everyone, but the proper amount in each case."[5]

He died at the age of about seventy.

---

[5] *Moralia,* Loeb Classical Library, Vol. II, p. 411.

6

MYSON

Philosopher noted for his Discernment

The last two of the Seven Greek Wise Men in Plato's list given in his *Protagoras*[1] — Myson and Chilon — were Spartans. Myson who flourished around 600 B.C., is mentioned sixth in the enumeration, Chilon last.

The native place of Myson was the village Chen. Its name means "goose." "Ch" stands for the 22nd letter of the Greek alphabet, the phonetic equivalent of which is the letter "H." The fact that Chen was a small and unimportant village, not a city, has resulted in the facts about Myson's life and thought remaining obscure. Thus, Diogenes Laertios has little to say about him — less than about any of the other Wise Men.

---

[1] 343A.

Though brief, Diogenes' account contains a very didactic anecdote and an important theory of truth. The anecdote, is as follows:

It is said that Anacharsis, who is reckoned by Plutarch and some other ancient writers as one of the Seven Wise Men — once went to the village of Chen in summer time and found Myson fitting a share to a plough and said: "Myson, this is not the season for the plough." To this, Myson remarked: "It is just the time to *repair* it."[2]

Plutarch himself makes the following comment regarding this anecdote: "Men should be *prepared* when they act, and not be making their preparations during the action, as Myson, who was fashioning a grainfork in wintertime, is reported to have remarked."[3]

Myson's theory of truth is contained in the following statement made by Diogenes: "He used to say that we should not investigate facts by the light of arguments, but arguments by the light of facts,

---

[2] Diogenes, *op. cit.*, I. 106-107.

[3] *Moralia*, Loeb Classical Library, Vol. IV, p. 129.

for the facts were not put together in order to fit the arguments, but the arguments to fit the facts."[4]

This is the substance of the classical theory of truth, known as "the correspondence theory," that was later developed by Socrates, Plato, and Aristotle, and is accepted by those who believe that truth is something objective, independent of our thinking, willing, etc. According to this view, a belief or proposition is true if it corresponds with the facts, with reality. It is false if it does not correspond with them.

In what he said about "facts" (*prágmata*) vs. "arguments" (*lógoi*), the Spartan was evidently criticizing those who endeavor to squeeze the facts into the mold of some preconception or hypothesis of theirs, thus reducing truth to something subjective, not reflecting the real order of things.

Myson died, according to Diogenes, at the age of ninety-seven.[5]

---

[4] *Op. cit.*, I. 108.

[5] *Ibid.*

7

CHILON

Magistrate and Poet

Chilon the Lacedaemonian (Spartan) was in his prime around 560 B.C., at which time he served as an Ephor (*Ephoros*) of Sparta. An Ephor there was one of a body of five magistrates who controlled even the kings. He acquired fame for his brevity of speech and wisdom. Diogenes credits Chilon with a poem in elegiac meter of some 200 lines and with many wise precepts.[1] Among the latter are the following:

"Control the tongue" (*Glóttes krateín*)."

"Do not use threats to anyone (*Me apeileín medení*)."

"Be more ready to visit friends in adversity than in prosperity."

"Honor old age (*Géras timán*)."

---

[1] *Op. cit.*, I, 68-70.

"Guard yourself (*Phylátein heautón*)." This may be taken to mean that we ought to watch our thoughts, feelings, desires, etc., lest they lead us to do what is wrong, evil.

"Prefer loss to dishonest gain." This is reminiscent of the view later advanced by Socrates that "It is better to suffer injustice than to do injustice."[2]

Chilon added to his saying, that loss will cause you sorrow once, while dishonest gain will cause sorrow forever. This statement shows that the Spartans had an active conscience, one that accused them when they did something immoral.

"Do not laugh at another's misfortune."

"Learn to be master of your own house."

"Let not your tongue get ahead of your mind (*Ten glóttan me protréchein tou nou*)."

"Control anger."

"Do not desire impossibilities."

"Do not hurry on the road." Aristotle was quite in agreement with Chilon on this matter. In his *Nichomachean Ethics* he remarks: "The great souled man (*megalópsychos*) is characterized by a slow gate,

---

[2] *Republic*, I.

a deep voice, and deliberate utterance. To speak in shrill tones and walk fast are characteristics of an excitable and nervous temperament."[3]

"Gesticulation in speaking should be avoided as a mark of madness."

"Obey the laws (*Nómois peíthesthai*)."

"Be calm (*Eremía chrésthai*)."

Chilon is said to have died in old age, after he had congratulated his son on an Olympic victory in boxing. In the light of what Solon said to Croesus regarding the happy man, he would have reckoned Chilon among the truly blessed men, because his earthly life had such a happy ending.

[3] IV. 1125a10-16.

8

ΡΗΤΑ ΤΩΝ ΕΠΤΑ ΣΟΦΩΝ ΘΗΣΑΥΡΙΣΜΕΝΑ ΥΠΟ ΑΓ. ΝΕΚΤΑΡΙΟΥ

ΘΑΛΗΣ

1. Κάλλιστος ὁ κόσμος· ποίημα γὰρ Θεοῦ.

2. Ἀγάπα τὸν πλησίον μικρὰ ἐλαττούμενος.

3. Τίς εὐδαίμων; Ὁ τὸ μὲν σῶμα ὑγιής, τὴν δὲ ψυχὴν εὔπορος, τὴν δὲ φύσιν εὐπαίδευτος.

4. Σοφώτατον χρόνος· ἀνευρίσκει γὰρ τὰ πάντα.

5. Σαφέστατος ἔλεγχος πραγμάτων ἁπάντων ἐστὶν ὁ χρόνος· οὗτος γὰρ τὴν ἀλήθειαν ἐμφανίζει.

6. Καιρὸν γνῶθι· ὀξὺς γάρ.

ΠΙΤΤΑΚΟΣ

1. Ἀρχὴ τὸν ἄνδρα δείκνυσι.

2. Μὴ πᾶσι πίστευε.

3. Δίδασκε καὶ μάνθανε τὸ ἄμεινον.

8

SAYINGS OF THE SEVEN SAGES TREASURED BY ST. NECTARIOS

THALES

1. The universe is most beautiful, for it is a work of God.

2. Love the neighbor, humbling yourself a little.

3. Who is happy? He who is healthy in body, resourceful in soul, and of a nature that is well educated.

4. Time is wisest, for it brings all things to light.

5. Time is the clearest scrutinizer of all things; for it makes the truth manifest.

6. Know thine opportune time; for it passes away quickly.

PITTACOS

1. Office makes evident the character of a man.

2. Do not believe everyone.

3. Teach and learn what is better.

4. Οἵους ἂν ἐράνους ἐνέγκῃς τοῖς γονεῦσι, τούτους αὐτὸς ἐν τῷ γήρᾳ παρὰ τῶν τέκνων προσδέχου.

5. Συγγνώμη τιμωρίας ἀμείνων· τὸ μὲν ἡμέρου φύσεως, τὸ δὲ θηριώδους.

6. Ἄριστος οἶκός ἐστιν ὁ τῶν περισσῶν μηδενὸς δεόμενος, καὶ τῶν ἀναγκαίων μηδενὸς ἐνδεόμενος.

7. Πιστὸν οὐδὲν γλῶσσα διὰ στόματος λαλεῖ διχόμυθον ἔχουσα καρδίᾳ νόημα.

8. Γλῶσσα ὄργανον μὲν ἀγαθῶν, ὄργανον δὲ τῶν κακῶν τῶν μεγίστων.

9. Ἀργὸς μὴ ἴσθι μηδ᾽ ἂν πλουτῇς.

10. Ἀργὸς μὴ ἴσθι· ἀνιαρὸν ἀργία.

11. Μέτρῳ χρῶ.

ΒΙΑΣ

1. Βραδέως ἐγχείρει· ὃ δ᾽ ἂν ἄρξῃ διαβεβαιοῦ.

4. Whatever services you render to your parents, such you will receive in your old age from your children.

5. Forgiveness is better than punishment. For the first is a characteristic of a tame nature, the second of a brutish.

6. That home is best which needs nothing of things superfluous, and is in want of nothing necessary.

7. The tongue says nothing truthworthy from the mouth when there is an ambiguous thought in the heart.

8. The tongue is an instrument of things good, but also an instrument of the greatest evils.

9. Do not remain idle, even when you are rich.

10. Do not remain idle; for idleness is something boring.

11. Exercise moderation.

BIAS

1. Be slow to undertake an enterprise; but when you have begun persevere in it strongly.

2.Τόπων μεταβολαὶ οὔτε φρόνησιν διδάσκουσιν οὔτε ἀφροσύνην ἀφαιροῦνται. Οἱ φρονοῦντες εὖ κρατοῦσι πανταχοῦ.

3. Αἰσχρὸν μὲν ἐν ἄλλοις ἀποδέχεσθαι τὰς ἀρετάς, ἐν ἑαυτοῖς δὲ ἔχειν τὰς κακίας.

4. Ἀστοῖσιν ἄρεσκε πᾶσιν ἐν πόλει· πλείστην γὰρ ἔχει χάριν. Αὐθάδης δὲ τρόπος βλαβερὰν ἐξέλαμψεν ἧτταν.

5. Μακάριός ἐστιν ὁ πλουτῶν, καὶ ὧν ἐπιθυμεῖ ἀπολαύων, ὁ δὲ μὴ ἐπιθυμῶν μακαριώτατος.

ΣΟΛΩΝ

1. Σόλων ὁ σοφὸς ἐκείνην εἶπεν ἄριστα οἰκεῖσθαι τὴν πόλιν, ἐν ᾗ τοὺς ἀγαθοὺς συμβαίνει τιμᾶσθαι· κάκιστα δὲ οἰκεῖσθαι, ἐν ᾗ τοὺς κακούς.

2. Ἐρωτηθεὶς ὁ Σόλων πῶς ἥκιστα ἀδικοῖεν οἱ ἄνθρωποι, εἰ ὁμοίως, ἔφη, ἄχθοιντο τοῖς ἀδικουμένοις οἱ μὴ ἀδικούμενοι.

2. Changes of places neither teach wisdom nor do they free a person from folly. It is those who think soundly that prevail everywhere.

3. It is shameful to approve of the virtues of others, but to have within oneself the vices.

4. Be agreeable to all the citizens in the city; for this wins favor. But an uncourteous manner often flashes forth harmful defeat.

5. Blessed is he who is rich and enjoys the things he desires; but he who is free from desires is the most blessed.

SOLON

1. Solon the wise man said that the city which is best governed is the one in which the virtuous are honored; and that is the worst governed in which the bad are honored.

2. Having been asked how men might cause as little injustice as possible, Solon replied: When those who do not suffer injustice are as much vexed by acts of injustice as are those who suffer injustice.

3. Πολλοὶ γὰρ πλουτοῦσι κακοί, ἀγαθοὶ δὲ πένονται. Ἀλλ᾽ ἡμεῖς αὐτοῖς οὐ διαμειψόμεθα τῆς ἀρετῆς τὸν πλοῦτον· ἐπεὶ τὸ μὲν ἔμπεδον ἀεί, χρήματα δὲ ἀνθρώπων ἄλλοτε ἄλλος ἔχει.

4. Μηδέποτ᾽ ὀρεχθῇς κτήσασθαι φίλον τὸν μήτε ψυχὴν μήτε σῶμα εὖ ποιῆσαι δυνάμενον.

5. Φίλους εὐσέβει.

6. Φίλους μὴ ταχὺ κτῶ, οὓς δ᾽ ἂν κτήσῃ, μὴ ταχὺ δ᾽ ἀποδοκίμαζε.

7. Μὴ εἴπῃς ποτὲ κακὸν διὰ τοὺς ἀποθανόντας.

8. Ἐσθλὴν περὶ αὐτοῦ δόξαν ἕκαστος ἔχει.

9. Ὡς κακὰ πολλὰ πόλει δυσνομία παρέχει.

10. Ἡδονὴ ἀθέμιτος βεβαίαν τίκτει λύπην. Ἡδονὴν φεῦγε, ἥτις λύπην τίκτει.

11. Εἰ δὲ πεπόνθατε λυγρὰ δι᾽ ὑμετέραν κακότητα, μή τι θεοῖς τούτων μοῖραν ἐπαμφέρετε.

12. Χρήματα δ᾽ ἱμείρω μὲν ἔχειν, ἀδίκως δὲ πεπᾶσθαι οὐκ ἐθέλω.

13. Γηράσκω δ᾽ ἀεὶ πολλὰ διδασκόμενος.

3. Many wicked men are rich, while virtuous men are poor. But we will not exchange the wealth of virtue with their riches; for the wealth of virtue is everlasting, whereas human riches are ever changing their owners.

4. Never desire to acquire a friend who can benefit neither the soul nor the body.

5. Act piously towards your friends.

6. Do not acquire friends quickly; and those whom you acquire do not quickly reject.

7. Never say anything bad about the deceased.

8. Every one has a good opinion about himself.

9. Lawlessness results in many evils in a city.

10. Lawless pleasure generates certain sorrow. Flee from pleasure that generates sorrow.

11. If you have suffered baneful things due to your wickedness, do not hold the gods responsible for these.

12. I desire to have goods, but to acquire them unjustly I do not want.

13. Ever, as I grow older, I learn more and more.

ΚΛΕΟΒΟΥΛΟΣ

1. Ἀρχὴ σοφίας τῆς ἀγνοίας ἡ γνῶσις.

2. Εἰς τὸ μὲν εὐπλοῆσαι κυβερνήτου καὶ πνεύματος χρεία, εἰς δὲ τὸ εὐδαιμονῆσαι λογισμοῦ καὶ τύχης.

3. Εὐτυχῶν μέτριος ἴσθι, ἀτυχῶν δὲ φρόνιμος.

4. Φαῦλος ἀνὴρ πίθος ἐστὶ τετρημένος, εἰς ὃν ἁπάσας ἀντλῶν τὰς χάριτας εἰς κενὸν ἐξέχεας.

5. Ἀνδρῶν ἀρίστων μνήμην πᾶσα ἡ πόλις γεραίρει.

6. Δεῖ συνοικίζειν ἀνδράσι τὰς ἑαυτῶν θυγατέρας, τὴν μὲν ἡλικίαν παρθένους, τὸ δὲ φρονεῖν γυναῖκας.

7. Γαμεῖν ἐκ τῶν ὁμοίων· ἐὰν γὰρ ἐκ τῶν κρειττόνων, δεσπότην, οὐ γυναῖκα κτήσῃ.

8. Οὔτε συμπόσιον ἄνευ ὁμιλίας, οὔτε πλοῦτος ἄνευ ἀρετῆς ἡδονὴν ἔχει.

CLEOBULOS

1. The beginning of wisdom consists in the knowledge of one's ignorance.

2. For a good voyage it is necessary that there be a good helmsman and wind, while for happiness one needs reason and good fortune.

3. When you are well off exercise moderation, when not, exercise wisdom.

4. A bad man is a perforated large wine-jar, pouring into which all the favors, you have poured them out into the void.

5. The memory of excellent men is honored by every city.

6. Men should give their daughters in marriage as virgins in body and mature women in mind.

7. A man should marry a woman similar to him in status; for if he marries one who is superior, he will acquire an absolute ruler and not a woman.

8. A feast without conversation is devoid of joy, so is wealth without virtue.

9. Μυστήριά σου μὴ κατείπῃς τῷ φίλῳ, καὶ οὐ φοβηθήσῃ αὐτὸν ἐχθρὸν γενόμενον.

10. Ἐρωτηθεὶς τίνα δεῖ μάλιστα φυλάττεσθαι; εἶπε, τῶν μὲν φίλων τὸν φθόνον, τῶν δ' ἐχθρῶν τὴν ἐπιβουλὴν· τῶν καὶ ἀρετῇ ζώντων ὁ τῆς λοιδορίας μῶμος οὐχ ἅπτεται.

11. Ἡ χάρις ἡ βραδύπους ἄχαρις χάρις.

12. Κλεόβουλος ἔφη φιλήκοον εἶναι μᾶλλον ἢ φιλόλαον.

13. Αἱ συμφοραὶ καὶ τὸν ἄγαν σώφρονα πολλάκις ἐξήγαγον ἀφεῖναι τι ῥῆμα τῶν αὐτοῦ τρόπων ἀνάξιον.

14. Ὅταν τις ἐξίῃ τῆς οἰκίας ζητείτω πρότερον τί μέλλει πράξειν, εἰσελθὼν δὲ τί ἔπραξεν.

9. Do not give an account of your secrets to your friend, and you will not have to fear that he might become your enemy.

10. Having been asked with regard to what one should be especially on one's guard, Cleobulos replied: With regard to the envy of one's friends and the plots of one's enemies; but those who live virtuously are not affected by the abuse of blame.

11. Favor that is slow in being given is favorless favor.

12. Cleobulos said that one should be fond of hearing rather than of speaking.

13. Misfortunes often have excited even those who are very self-controlled to say something unbecoming for them.

14. When one steps out of his home he should first ask himself what he intends to do, and when he enters it he should ask himself what he has done.

ΜΥΣΩΝ

Μύσων ὁ Χηνεὺς ἔφασκε μὴ ἐκ τῶν λόγων τὰ πράγματα, ἀλλ᾽ ἐκ τῶν πραγμάτων τοὺς λόγους ζητεῖν· οὐ γὰρ ἕνεκα τῶν λόγων τὰ πράγματα συντελεῖσθαι, ἀλλ᾽ ἕνεκα τῶν πραγμάτων τοὺς λόγους.

ΧΕΙΛΩΝ

1. Χείλων ἐρωτηθείς, τί τὸ χαλεπώτερον; τὸ γινώσκειν ἑαυτὸν ἔφη. Χρήσιμον γὰρ εἰς νουθεσίαν τῶν ἀλαζόνων, οἵπερ τὴν ἑαυτῶν δύναμιν φλυαροῦσι.

2. Τὸν τετελευτηκότα μὴ κακολόγει, ἀλλὰ μακάριζε.

3. Γάμους εὐτελεῖς καὶ ἰσοτίμους ποιοῦ.

4. Τοῖς πλουτοῦσι μάλιστα παρέπεσθαι φιλεῖ τὸ δυσήνιον, καὶ ἐκ πλείστης ἀγερωχίας, κατασύρονται εἰς τὸ ράθυμον.

5. Ἐπὶ τὰ δεῖπνα τῶν φίλων βραδέως πορεύου, ἐπὶ δὲ τὰς ἀτυχίας ταχέως.

MYSON

Myson of Chen used to say that we should not investigate facts by the light of arguments, but arguments by the light of facts. For the facts were not put together in order to fit the arguments, but the arguments to fit the facts.

CHILON

1. Chilon was asked what is the most difficult thing. He answered: To know oneself. Self-knowledge is valuable for the boastful, who babble about their power.

2. Do not speak ill of one deceased, rather call him blessed.

3. Make wedding feasts that are thrifty and appropriate to your status.

4. The rich are especially accompanied by waywardness, and by their great arrogance they lapse into heedlessness.

5. Proceed slowly to the feasts of your friends, but hasten to them in their misfortunes.

6. Πρεσβύτερον σέβου.

7. Ἡ γλῶσσα μὴ προτρέχου τῆς διανοίας. Ἡ γλῶσσα πολλοὺς εἰς ὄλεθρον ἤγαγεν· εἰ μὴ καθέξῃς γλῶσσαν, ἔσται σοι κακά.

8. Εἰ τὰ κακὰ πάντων κατανοήσεις, ἧττον ἐπὶ τοῖς σεαυτοῦ δυσφορήσεις.

9. Ἀδικούμενος διαλλάσσου, ὑβριζόμενος δὲ μὴ τιμωροῦ.

10. Ζημίαν αἱρεῖσθαι μᾶλλον ἢ κέρδος αἰσχρόν· ἡ μὲν γὰρ ἅπαξ ἐλύπησε, τὸ δὲ διὰ παντός.

6. Show reverence for the elderly.

7. Let not your tongue get ahead of your mind. The tongue has led many to destruction. If you do not bridle your tongue, many evils will befall you.

8. If you observe well the misfortunes of all others, you will bear yours with less pain.

9. When you suffer injustice, be reconciled, when you are insulted do not exact vengeance.

10. Prefer loss to disgraceful gain; for the first causes sorrow once, the second forever.

BIBLIOGRAPHY

Aristotle, *Eudemian Ethics, Nichomachean Ethics, Politics, The Constitution of Athens,* in The Loeb Classical Library, Cambridge, Massachusetts: Harvard University Press.

Athenagoras the Athenian Philosopher and Christian Apologist, *A Plea for the Christians,* in *The Ante-Nicene Fathers,* Vol. II, Grand Rapids, Michigan: Wm. B. Eerdmans Publishing Company.

Basil the Great, Saint, *To Young Men on How They Might Profit from Greek Literature,* in The Loeb Classical Library, Vol. IV of Basil's *Letters.*

Burnet, John, *Early Greek Philosophy.* London, 1920.

Clement of Alexandria, *Stromata,* in *The Ante-Nicene Fathers,* Vol. II.

Diogenes Laertius, *Lives and Opinions of Eminent Philosophers,* in The Loeb Classical Library, Vol. I.

Freeman, Kathleen, *The Work and Life of Solon.* Cardiff, 1926.

Freeman, Kathleen, *The Pre-Socratic Philosophers.* Cambridge, Massachusetts and Oxford, 1946.

Herodotus, *History,* in The Loeb Classical Library, Vol. I.

Kontoglou, Photios, *Ekphrasis tes Orthodoxou Eikonographias* ("Explanation of Orthodox Iconography"), Vol. I., Athens, 1960.

Linforth, Ivan Mortimer, *Solon the Athenian: Biographical Essay and Fragments of Solon's Poem.* Berkeley, California, 1919.

Nectarios Kephalas, Metropolitan of Pentapolis, *Hieron kai Philosophikon Logion Thesaurisma* ("Treasury of Sacred and Philosophical Sayings"), Vols. 1 and 2. Athens, 1895-1896.

Nectarios Kephalas, *Peri tes Alethous kai Pseudous Morphoseos* ("Concerning True and Pseudo Education"). Athens, 1894.

Plato, *Charmides, Critias, Laches, Laws, Phaedrus, Protagoras, Republic, Theaetetus,Timaeus,* in The Loeb Classical Library.

Plutarch, "Solon," in *Lives,* Vol. I, The Loeb Classical Library.

Plutarch, "Symposium of the Seven Wise Men," in *Moralia,* Vol. II, The Loeb Classical Library.

Russell, Bertrand, *A History of Western Philosophy.* New York, 1945.

Stobaeus, Ioannes, *Anthologium,* Vol. II, Berlin, 1884.

Sociades, *Ton Hepta Sophon kai ton syn Autois Katarithmoumenon Apophthegmata, Symboulai, kai Hypothekai* ("Apophthegms, Counsels, and Suggestions of the Seven Sages and of Those Reckoned Among Them"). Paris, 1554.

Thomas, Ivor, trans., "Thales," in *Greek Mathematics,* Vol. I, The Loeb Classical Library.

Zeller, Edward, *Outlines of the History of Greek Philosophy.* London and New York, 1895.

INDEX OF PROPER NAMES

INDEX OF SUBJECTS

Index of Subjects